My HEART MATTERS

A CHILD'S 10 DAY JOURNEY WITH JESUS

WRITTEN BY JO NAUGHTON

ILLUSTRATED BY MARY-GRACE MACHARIA

GHP

Grosvenor House
Publishing Limited

MY **HEART** MATTERS

DAY 6

LET'S PRAY

MY **HEART** MATTERS

DAY 4

DAY 9

LET'S PRAY

DAY 10

SUPER DAD

MY **HEART** MATTERS

MY **HEART** MATTERS

LET'S PRAY

DAY 3

DAY 8

MY HEART MATTERS

DAY 1

LET'S P

DAY 5

Peace

MY HEART MATTERS

DAY 7

HEA MAT

DAY 2

The right of Jo Naughton to be identified as the author of this
work has been asserted in accordance with Section 78
of the Copyright, Designs and Patents Act 1988

The book cover and all illustrations are
copyright to Mary Grace Macharia

This book is published by
Grosvenor House Publishing Ltd
Link House
140 The Broadway, Tolworth, Surrey, KT6 7HT.
www.grosvenorhousepublishing.co.uk

A CIP record for this book
is available from the British Library

ISBN 978-1-80381-957-0

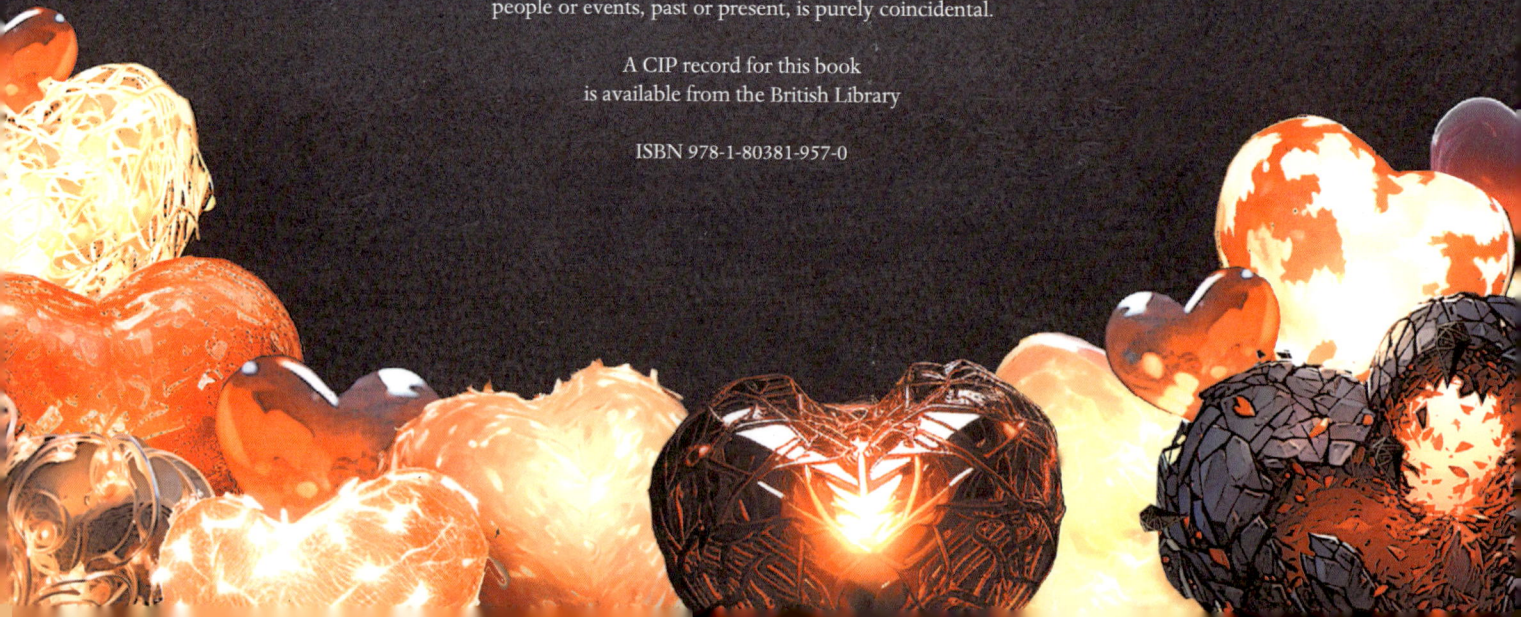

DAY 1
MY HEART

"Guard your heart above all else, for it determines the course of your life."
Proverbs 4:23 (NLT)

You are very precious. When God created you, He made you just like Him.
That means your heart is like God's heart.

God's heart is gigantic! He is full to overflowing with love for you. Because He loves you, He has lots of other feelings too. When wonderful things happen to you, He is happy. When horrible things happen to you, He is sad. When people are kind to you, He is glad. When people are cruel to you, He gets upset. God gave you different feelings too, and He cares about the way you feel, He cares about what you think.

God wants your heart to feel light and happy!

Which feelings have you had today?
What made you feel that way?

God doesn't want you to be sad or lonely. He doesn't want you to be scared or upset. Any time you feel bad, God wants to make you feel better.
He wants you to know that you can talk to Him about anything.
He cares about you so He loves it when you tell Him how you're feeling.

"Pour out your heart like water to the Lord."
Lamentations 2:19 (NLT)

Your heart is precious and fragile, a bit like glass.

Feelings are a bit like butterflies, they need to be set free. The way you set your feelings free is by talking to Jesus. Tell Him how you feel and let Him know if anything is bothering you. He wants to hear about your day. He loves to listen to you.

Did you know that it was God who gave you the ability to cry? Crying is another way you can release your feelings. You can cry while you talk to Jesus. He loves you and He will never leave you on your own.

How To Pray When Horrible Things Happen.
Find a quiet place where you can be alone.
Tell Jesus what happened and how it made you feel.
If you feel like crying, cry while you are with Jesus.
Picture Jesus right beside you.

Feelings are like butterflies, they need to be set free.

LET'S PRAY

Heavenly Father,

I open up my heart to You. If there are any feelings trapped inside, please help me to let them go. I want to tell you about my day...

(Share what happened and how you felt. Tell Jesus about the good things and tell Him about the bad things.)

Thank You that You love me. Thank You that You will never leave me on my own. Thank You that I can talk to You about anything, any time I want. I love You.

In Jesus' name I pray,

Amen.

When you invite Jesus in, He lights up your heart

Day 2
WORDS THAT HURT

"Kind words heal and help; cutting words hurt people..."
Proverbs 15:4

God made the whole world with His words! He said, Let there be light!"
and suddenly the earth and sky were filled with light.
Can you imagine that? When God wanted to make fish and birds,
He spoke Swarm, ocean, with fish and all sea life!
Birds, fly through the sky over earth!" God created the huge whales,
all the swarm of life in the waters, and every kind... of flying birds...
(Genesis 1:20-21 MSG)

God spoke from His heart when He created world

On Day 1, we learned that God made you and me like Him.
That means that our words are powerful, just like His.
Kind words make you happy, they make you feel good about yourself.

Encouraging words build your confidence, and help you remember
that you are smart and that you have what it takes to do well.

The bible is full wonderful statements about you. Scripture says
that you are a work of art, it says that you are God's masterpiece!
The bible explains that you achieve anything - when you do it with Jesus.

The Bible explains that when someone says nasty things,
it feels like being stabbed. Words can't make you bleed,
but they can hurt your feelings. When people say ugly things.
it can make you feel horrible.

Reading God's word
makes you happy

Mean words can hurt your feelings and make you feel small.
When I was at school, a teacher said that I was awful at reading. He called
me stupid in front of a room of people. It made me feel stupid and made me
ashamed of myself. It made me hate reading.

Has anyone at school said anything mean to you?
Has your brother, sister or a friend called you names?
Has anyone else said anything that hurt?

Jesus doesn't want you to feel bad. He doesn't want you to think you're
stupid. He wants to heal your heart. If you get a splinter in your finger,
someone will need to take it out. This stops it getting infected.
When nasty things are said to you, they can be like splinters.

Jesus wants to take those words out of your heart. Jesus does
not want you to believe the cruel things that people have said.
He wants you to know that you are smart and you are special.

Cruel words hurt, they can make your heart feel dark

HOW TO PRAY WHEN PEOPLE SAY MEAN THINGS

Find a quiet place where you can be alone.
Tell Jesus what they said and how it made you feel.
While you tell Him, He will take those words out of your heart.
If you feel like crying, cry while you are with Jesus.
Jesus says you are smart, Jesus says you are special.
Now say out loud 'I am smart. I am special. Jesus loves me just as I am.'

LET'S PRAY

Heavenly Father,

People have said things that hurt my feelings.
Maybe they didn't mean to be unkind, but their words hurt me.
(Share what happened and how you felt.
Tell Jesus about the good things and tell him about the bad things)
Thank You, Lord, for taking these words out of my heart. Thank You that I am like You. That means I am smart. It means I am special. Thank You that You love me.
Thank You that I can talk to You about anything, anytime I want.

I love You, Lord. In Jesus' name, I pray,

Amen.

When God heals your heart, it will feel light again

DAY 3
FIGHTS

"The rage and anger of others can be overwhelming"
Proverbs 27:4

God wants you to feel safe. He never wants you to be scared. But things happen that are frightening. You may have had a hard time at home, at school or when you went out. Jesus cares about how you feel and He wants to help.

DIFFERENT TYPES OF FIGHTS

Fights can be frightening. Sometimes children have arguments, sometimes adults quarrel, sometimes grown-ups get cross with children. When people are angry, it can be scary. It feels good when everyone is happy and calm. But when people shout, it is horrible. When doors slam or things bang, it is upsetting.

God wants you to feel safe, like you're wrapped in His heart

Anytime you are afraid, Jesus will be right beside you. He will never leave you on your own. Jesus is strong and kind, and He loves you very much. You can't see Jesus, but you can picture Him beside you. You might even be able to sense Him in your heart - it's like a happy feeling inside. Even if you can't feel anything, He is with you.

Shut your eyes right now and picture Jesus beside you.
Ask Him to wrap you up in His love.

Jesus is always right beside you.

ANGRY TIMES

When I was a child, my dad sometimes got angry and shouted.
It made me upset. Has anyone got angry with you?
Have you been frightened or hurt?

If you have gone through things that made you sad, please don't push your feelings down. If you are upset about something that has happened, talk to Jesus. Tell Him what happened and how it made you feel. He wants to heal your precious heart.

It can feel frightening when people shout

How To Pray After Shouting Or Fights

Find a quiet place where you can be alone.
Tell Jesus what happened and how it made you feel.
If you feel like crying, cry while you are with Jesus.
Jesus says, I love you very much and I'm here for you.

Let's Pray

Heavenly Father,

People sometimes get angry and it upsets me. I don't like it when they shout or when things bang. It makes me scared and sad.

(Now tell the Lord about anything you have remembered. Tell Him what happened and how it made you feel)

Thank You, Jesus, that You are strong and You love me. Thank You, Lord, that You are beside me right now. Please fill my heart with Your love. Please fill my heart with Your peace. Thank You that You will never leave me on my own.

Thank You that I can talk to You about anything, anytime I want.

I love You, Lord. In Jesus' name, I pray,

Amen.

When God heals your heart, it will feel light again

DAY 4
FEELING LEFT OUT

"Of all the people on earth, the Lord your God has chosen you to be his own special treasure."

Deuteronomy 7:6

God has far too much love to keep to Himself! He made you so that He could share His affection. His plan was for you to enjoy constant kindness. He wanted you to feel secure and happy all the time. He made your heart like a sponge so that you could soak up all His wonderful love.

God never makes mistakes, but people do. God loves all the time, but humans are sometimes mean. Because your heart was made to soak up love, it hurts when people push you away.

God wants you to enjoy good friendships

The Bible tells the story of a dad called Jacob who had 12 sons. He loved one of his sons, Joseph, more than he loved his other children. This made Joseph's brothers feel bad. One day, their dad gave Joseph a beautiful coat. But he didn't give the other boys a present. This really hurt their feelings and made them angry.

PUSHED AWAY

We all feel left out sometimes. Maybe a teacher kept telling you off, even when you tried your best. Perhaps children at school left you out of their games. You might not have many friends. You could feel pushed away by your mom or dad. Your brother or sister may have made fun of you. Perhaps people have put you down because of the way you look, where you're from, or even the color of your skin. Most people feel unwanted sometimes and it feels horrible.

Joseph was his dad's favorite, his brothers felt left out

When people push you away, it can make you think that you're not as good as other people. It can make you think you're not very nice or not very smart. You might even think that it was your fault. Please don't listen to any voice inside telling you lies like these.

Jesus does not want you to feel like you're less important than anyone else. He does not want you to feel bad about yourself. He does not want you to be sad or lonely. Did you know that it hurts Jesus when you are hurting?

Jeremiah 8: 21

explains, "I hurt with the hurt of my people..."
Jesus wants to take your pain away and He wants
you to know that you are very, very special.

When people leave you out,
it can make you feel bad

God war

Him h

How to Pray After People Push You Away

Find a quiet place where you can be alone.
Tell Jesus how you feel and tell Him about anything you have
gone through that hurt your feelings.
If you want to cry, you can cry.
Jesus says, I picked you. I chose you. I love you. You belong to My family.
Let those words sink into your heart.

Let's Pray

Heavenly Father,

Sometimes people push me away and it makes me feel awful. I don't know why they don't want me to be close to them. It hurts my feelings and makes me think I'm not good enough.

(Now tell the Lord about anything specific that happened that hurt you. Tell Him what happened and how it made you feel)

I ask You to heal my heart. Thank You, Jesus, that You chose me. Thank You, Lord, that You picked me. I'm so glad that You love me very much and I belong to Your family. Thank You that I am already good enough because You designed me. I will never be on my own because You are always beside me.

Thank You that I can talk to You about anything, anytime I want.

I love You, Lord. In Jesus' name, I pray,

Amen.

ou to tell
you feel

DAY 5
It Feels Like It's My Fault

"Give all your worries and cares to God, for he cares about you."
1 Peter 5:7

Do you think that arguments at home are your fault? Do you wonder what you did wrong or how you can make things better? Maybe when adults are having quiet conversations, you worry that they are talking about you. Do you blame yourself when bad things happen?

God is very real! There is also a devil. It is the devil that makes horrible things happen. He is wicked and he is a liar (see John 8:44). He wants to blame you for bad things that he has done. He wants you to think that it's your fault when grown-ups make mistakes. Sometimes he whispers lies into your ears to make you feel responsible.

It is NOT your fault when horrible things happen. You are NOT responsible for things that other people say and do. The devil wants you to blame yourself, but Jesus wants you to know the truth: IT'S NOT YOUR FAULT.

When things go wrong, it can make you feel bad.

WORRY

Do you worry? Life is full of difficulties and perhaps it feels too much. Are you worried about anything at home? Are you anxious about what is happening at school? Maybe someone is sick or your family has problems. You might be concerned for a friend.

Worry is horrible. Nagging thoughts go round and round your head and your tummy churns. But worry never makes anything better. It only ever makes things worse.

Jesus doesn't want you to worry about anything. He cares about you and He is very good at solving problems. So He wants you to give Him all your concerns.

worry feels horrible!

How To Give God Your Worries

Find a quiet space where you can be alone.
Tell Jesus what you are worried about. Tell Him all about it.
If you thought any bad things were your fault, tell Jesus.
If you want to cry, cry while you are talking to Jesus.
Tell God that you are giving Him all your worries and problems!

When you give God your worries,
you will feel lighter

LET'S PRAY

Heavenly Father,

Sometimes I feel like problems are my fault. Sometimes I feel bad when horrible things happen, I thought that I was the problem. But now I know that I'm not to blame. It's NOT my fault!

Sometimes I worry. It makes me feel awful.

(Are you worried about anything at the moment? If so, tell Jesus what is worrying you and how you are feeling. Tell Him all about it.)

Thank You, Jesus, that You care about me. Thank You, Lord, that You care about the things that are important to me. I'm not going to worry anymore! Instead, I give You my worries, I hand every concern to You. I can't fix this, but You can work it out. So I let go, I give You ALL of my worries! I let them ALL go right now. Thank You that You are always right beside me.

Thank You that I can talk to You about anything, anytime I want.

I love You, Lord. In Jesus' name, I pray,

Amen.

It's NOT your fault

DAY 6
LETTiNG GO

"... If you have anything against anyone, forgive them..."
Mark 11:25

It is horrible when people are mean. That's why you need to give all your pain to Jesus. But there is something else that you need to do when you are hurt. We are going to learn today how to let go.

It is not fair when people are mean, so it can make you annoyed. If children at school call you names, you might be angry with them. If someone makes you scared, you may want them to feel bad too. If things go wrong, you might sulk.

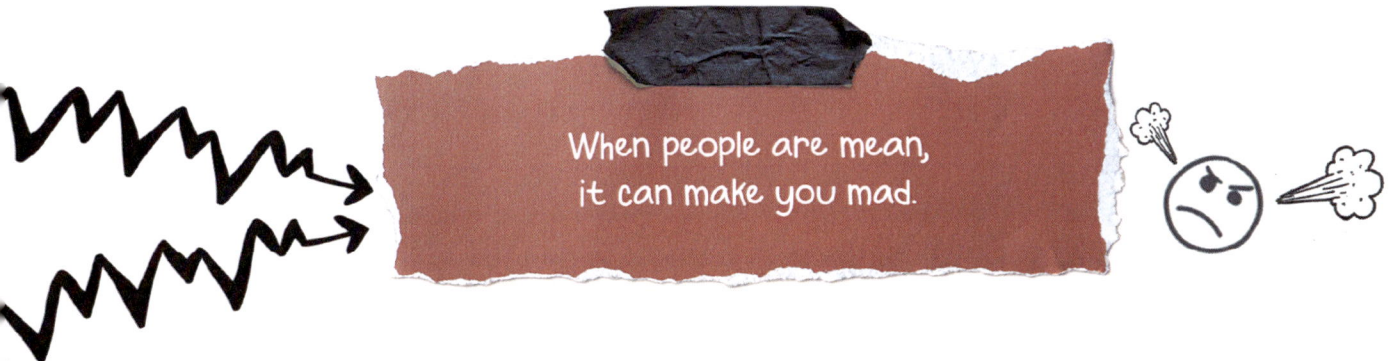

When people are mean,
it can make you mad.

Unforgiveness is when you are upset with someone who has hurt you. It is when you are annoyed with someone who did something wrong. They could have hurt you or maybe they were unkind to someone you love.

Holding onto anger does not help. In fact, it makes things worse. You might feel bad every time you see them. Maybe you keep remembering what they said. Perhaps you get upset when they do well. Unforgiveness does not harm other people. It harms you.

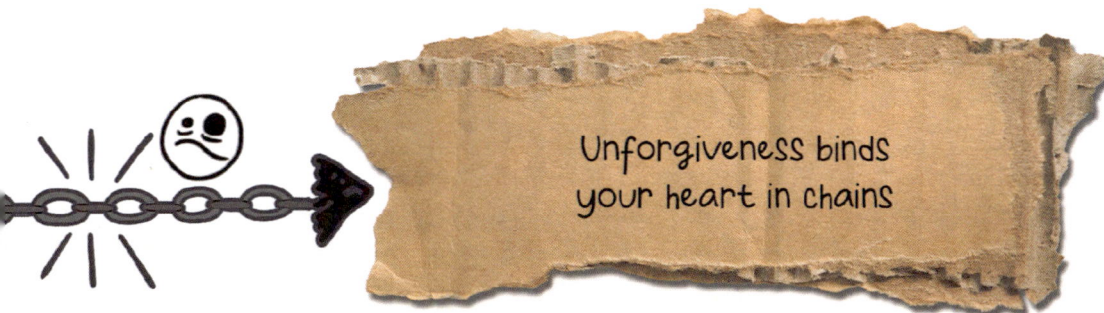

Unforgiveness binds your heart in chains

Jesus forgave the men who put Him on the cross. Even while He was in terrible pain, He prayed:

"… Father, forgive them, for they don't know what they are doing."

(Luke 23:34).

Think about some of the people who have made you feel bad. Have any teachers or children hurt your feelings? Has anyone at home upset you? What about other people that you know? Are you mad at anyone? Do you feel annoyed? You will feel great after you have let go!

HOW TO FORGIVE

Find a quiet space where you can be alone.
Tell Jesus who upset you and what they did.
Then tell Jesus that you are ready to let go of what they did wrong.
Say out loud, "I forgive .... (say their name) and I let go of my anger". Ask God to help the people who hurt you to be better people.

Jesus taught us how to let go

LET'S PRAY

Heavenly Father,

Sometimes people are mean. I have been hurt, but today I am going to forgive.

(Now bring each person who has upset you to God in prayer, one by one.)

I bring .... to You, Lord.

They hurt me and made me feel bad, but today I am going to let go.

I forgive .... for hurting my feelings. I don't want .... to pay for what they

did. I let go of my anger, Lord. I give You all my upset. I LET GO!

Lord, I ask you to help .... in any way that they need help.

Thank You, Lord, for setting me free from all those bad feelings!

I love You, Lord. In Jesus' name, I pray,

Amen.

When you forgive, your heart feels happy and light

IT DIDN'T HAPPEN

"When hope is crushed, the heart is crushed."

Proverbs 13:12

Have you ever been disappointed when you thought something good was about to happen, and it didn't? It's horrible, isn't it? It seems really unfair. You may end up feeling down in the dumps and sad. Sometimes, those feelings hang around for a long time.

When I was 12 years old, my grandfather died. Grandpa was probably the kindest man I had ever met. He used to take me for lovely walks and read me stories when I stayed at his house. When I heard that Grandpa had died, I burst into tears. My favorite person in the world was gone.

When things go wrong, it can make you feel bad

Has anything sad happened to you? Have you missed out on something that you were really looking forward to? It could be at school, with your family or among friends. Has anyone you love passed away? Have you lost any friends, or maybe even a pet?

When you are hoping that something good is going to happen, it can be very upsetting when it doesn't work out. It can make your heart sink. It can make you sad. Any time you are disappointed, Jesus wants to make you feel better.

When it doesn't work out
it can hurt.

The Bible tells us that God "...heals the wounds of every shattered heart." (Psalms 147:3). When a cut is healed, it doesn't hurt anymore. It's exactly the same with your heart. When something has hurt you, Jesus can take all your pain away. He wants to help you when your heart is broken, but He also wants to help when small things make you sad.

HOW TO PRAY WHEN YOU ARE DISAPPOINTED

Find a quiet space where you can be alone.
Tell Jesus exactly what happened and how it made you feel.
If you want to cry, cry while you are talking to Jesus.
Then give God the thing that feels unfair. Let it go.
Jesus says, "I love you and I have lots of surprises in store for you!"

God's word can heal your heart.

LET'S PRAY

Heavenly Father,

There are times when I have been hoping for something good to happen, and it all went wrong. Life sometimes feels unfair, Lord. It upsets me when things don't work out. It's hard, Lord.

(Now tell the Lord about any disappointments that have made you sad. Tell Him about any big things, but also about any small things that made you feel bad. Tell Him what happened and how it made you feel.)

Now I give You the thing that feels unfair. I give You the part that feels wrong. I let it go and hand my disappointment to You.

Thank You, Jesus, that You have lots of good things in store for me. Even when people let me down, You keep Your promises. Thank You, Lord, that You are beside me right now. Please fill my heart with Your love and Your joy.

Thank You that I can talk to You about anything, anytime I want.

I love You, Lord, In Jesus' name, I pray,

Amen.

When you give your sadness to God, your heart will feel light again

MY DAD

"See how very much our Father loves us, for he calls us his children, and that is what we are!"

1 John 3:1

What do you think God is like? Do you think He is strict? Do you think He is far away? Or do you think He is close? Do you imagine that God is happy and smiles? Or do you think He is angry most of the time? Here is a funny question: do you think God likes cuddles?

Most people think God is like their father. If your dad is always hugging you, you probably think God likes cuddles. If you don't know your dad, you might think God is far away. If your dad shouts a lot, you may think God gets angry easily.

SUPER DAD

God is the most wonderful Father ever!

Being a father or a mother is a very hard job! So every dad and every mom on earth makes mistakes. Even when they try their best, they will let you down. My dad didn't talk very much. He was quiet - unless he was angry. He never told me he loved me and I don't remember him giving me hugs.

God is the BEST father ever! He is so kind. He is gentle, even though He is super strong. Your Heavenly Father wants you to feel safe and secure all the time. He wants you to be happy. God doesn't get angry when you get things wrong. He has a big smile on His face when you come into His presence.

We can all be a part of God's family.

When you are upset, your Heavenly Father wants to make you feel better. He even enjoys singing songs to you! The Bible tells us: "With his love, He will calm all your fears. He will rejoice over you with joyful songs." (Zephaniah 3:17). Being with God is like enjoying the biggest, kindest cuddle in the world.

How To Receive The Love Of Your Heavenly Father

Find a quiet space where you can be alone.
Picture your Heavenly Father smiling at you.
He says, "You are my precious child. I love you SO much."
You reply, "Thank You for loving me! I love You too, Daddy God."
Sit quietly and picture your Heavenly Father close by your side.

When you feel your Heavenly Father's love, it will fill your heart with joy.

LET'S PRAY

Heavenly Father,

I never knew what You were really like. But now I realize that You are THE
BEST dad in the whole wide world. No one is as amazing as You!
(If you have been hurt by your dad or your mom - like we all have - tell the Lord
what happened and how it made you feel. Tell your Heavenly Father, then ask Him
to heal your heart and fill you with His love.)

Thank You Lord that You are interested in how I feel. You are interested in how I get
on at school and You are interested in all my friendships. Thank You that You love
me when I'm good and You love me when I'm naughty. You're not mad at me. You
don't get angry when I make mistakes.

Thank You for being so kind to me and for loving me all the time.

I love You too, Daddy God, and I receive Your love into my heart.

In Jesus' name, I pray,

Amen.

The Father's love will make
your heart feel light!

MY BIG BROTHER

"We now belong to His same Father, so He is not ashamed or embarrassed to introduce us as His brothers and sisters!"

Hebrews 2:11

You have an amazing big brother! He is super strong and very kind. He loves you with all of His heart and He is always by your side. Jesus is the BEST brother ever.

OUR EARTHLY FAMILY

Do you have a brother or sister? You might have lots of children growing up in your home or you may be an only child. If you have siblings, are you close to them? Do you have fun or do you fight a lot, or both? If you are an only child, do you ever feel lonely?

When God created family, He wanted you to enjoy the love of your parents and the friendship of your siblings. If you are always fighting with a brother or sister, it may make you feel sad or lonely. If that's you, God wants to heal your heart.

Jesus is the best big brother.

WHEN THINGS ARE HARD AT HOME

When I was a child, I wasn't very close to my brother or my sister. Because our family suffered a lot, things were often tense at home. When we grew up, we drifted apart. As an adult, I struggled to see Jesus as my big brother.

One day, God showed me that my distant relationship with my siblings had affected my relationship with Jesus.

When you fall out with friends or family, it can make your heart hurt.

How Jesus helped me...

I found a quiet space to pray and then I told the Lord that I was sad about
my relationship with my brother and sister. I cried as I prayed.
Afterwards, I felt Jesus come alongside me and put His arm around my shoulder.
For the first time ever, I felt His BIG BROTHER love. It was amazing! Now I cherish
the relationship I have with Jesus.

In John 15:15, Jesus said something very special: "...
I have called you friends..." Because He is your big brother.
He is also your friend. He enjoys spending time
with you and He loves it when you talk with Him.

Jesus wants to heal your heart
when relationships aren't working.

HOW TO PRAY WHEN YOU'RE SAD OR LONELY

Find a quiet space where you can be alone.
If you're hurt or lonely, tell Jesus how you feel.
If you want to cry, cry while you are talking to Jesus.
Now picture Jesus, your Big Brother, sitting beside you.
He says, "I love you and I will always be here for you."
You reply, "Thank You for being my Big Brother! I love You too, Jesus."

LET'S PRAY

Heavenly Father,

Thank You for Your love for me. Thank You for being kind to me and for loving me so much that You gave me Jesus.

(If you have been hurt by friends or siblings, tell the Lord what happened and how it made you feel. If you're lonely, tell Jesus why and share your feelings.)

Thank You, Jesus, for being my amazing BIG BROTHER. Thank You for loving me and staying by my side at all times. I am so happy that You call me Your friend. Wow, what a privilege to be a friend of Yours!
I receive Your BIG BROTHER love into my heart. I love You too!

I love You, Lord. In Jesus' name, I pray,

Amen.

Jesus' big brother love feels.... AMAZING!

DAY 10
MY AMZAZING FRIEND

"The Friend, the Holy Spirit..."
Proverbs 27:4

God the Father, God the Son and God the Holy Spirit are One. A triangle has three sides, but it is one shape. In the same way, God is three, but One. They are family and They love each other very much.

When Jesus went to heaven, our Father sent the Holy Spirit to earth to be with His children, and that includes you. He is AMAZING and He wants to be close to you in lots of different ways.

God's heart is HUGE and FILLED with love.

LET'S GET TO KNOW HIM

The Holy Spirit is your helper. When you don't know what to do, He wants to help. He is your guide, When you are stuck, the Holy Spirit can show you what to do. The Holy Spirit is your friend. You can talk to Him about anything. He will never leave you on your own and He will never let you down. He loves to talk to you too.

He is the best ever Comforter. Anytime you are sad or lonely, He wants to make you feel better. He wants to be close to you. His presence feels like the kindest cuddle ever.

The Holy Spirit is also super strong and very powerful! There is nothing too difficult for Him. When He fills you with His presence, you can be strong and powerful too!

The Holy Spirit wants to be close to you ALWAYS!

Peace

FILLED TO OVERFLOWING

The Holy Spirit wants to pour His love into your heart and fill you to overflowing with His power. He wants you to enjoy peace and calm, even when things are difficult. He wants to fill you with joy which will bubble up inside.

HOW TO INVITE THE HOLY SPIRIT TO FILL YOUR HEART

Find a quiet space where you can be alone.
Ask the Father to pour the Holy Spirit into your heart.
Lift up your hands like you are receiving a gift.
Say, "I receive You, Holy Spirit, into my heart and life!"
Sit still and enjoy receiving His power and joy into your heart.

The Holy Spirit fills your heart up with His love

LET'S PRAY

Heavenly Father,

Thank You for sending the Holy Spirit to be with us, Your children.
I open up my heart and I ask You to fill me to overflowing with the Holy Spirit now.
I ask You to pour Your presence and Your power into my life. I receive Your love,
I receive Your joy, I receive Your comfort, I receive Your help, I receive You as my
amazing Friend.

Thank You, Holy Spirit, for filling my heart and life. Thank You that You will never
leave me on my own. Thank You that You will help me anytime I ask. Thank You
that You will comfort me anytime I'm hurting.
I am SO grateful for Your love and Your presence. You are the BEST friend I could
ever have. Please help me to follow Jesus all my life.

Thank You, Lord, that You love me. I love You too!

In Jesus' name, I pray,
Amen.

Your Friend, the Holy Spirit will be with you wherever you go.

MY HEART MATTERS

DAY 6

LET'S PRAY

MY HEART MATTERS

DAY 4

DAY 9

LET'S PRAY

DAY 10

SUPER DAD

MY HEART MATTERS

MY HEART MATTERS

LET'S PRAY

S PRAY

DAY 3

DAY 8

MY HEART MATTERS

DAY 1

DAY 5

LET'S PR

Peace

My HEART MATTERS

DAY 7

HEA MATT

DAY 2

www.ingramcontent.com/pod-product-compliance
Lightning Source LLC
Chambersburg PA
CBRC090824100426
42812CB00021B/2668